why i never got to neptune

Ptarmigan House
Maryland, USA

Cover design by Victoria Heath Silk (VictoriaHeathSilk.com)
Book design & typesetting by Studio26 (insidestudio26.com)

Why i never got to neptune and other poems/Stewart Hickman. -- 1st ed.
ISBN 979-8-9857393-3-6 (paperback)
ISBN 979-8-9857393-4-3 (ebook)

why i never got to neptune

and other poems

Stewart Hickman

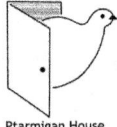

Ptarmigan House

to Busy Graham

Contents

places

people

perspective

why i never got to neptune

pla**ces**

Astana Park

Your step is slow in Astana Park.
The path uneven concrete pads,
the fountains capped for winter just past.
Now the grass brightens,
the piles of leaves are put in bags,
in clusters under the spruce,
and lengths and lengths of roses wait;
groups of thorny sticks ringed by busts of dirt.
On each bench is perched a couple;
this one, he sits, her head on his lap.
No one is alone this spring day,
dad holds a sleeping child,
mom walks with daughter whose black hair
is half her height.
A man standing reads, pushes the pram
gently to and fro;
she sleeps, he reads, looks at her,
then reads again.
Traffic races on the sides of the park,
surrounding these trees, these roses, these parents
these lovers, all dappled in the tiniest of bird songs
as though we could all be here a long time.

Waves at Pattaya

Here is a kilometer of gulf shore
south of the distant hand of smog
pressing the city to its surfaces, and
north of the morning farmer

with the sorry dogs
who waits by his wisp of smoke
to wave to a walker-by.
At night I am pulled to the wave-side,

darkness roaring around me.
The moon is over my head.
The sea does not so much end
as push without cease against this place.

A bird clacks once from the shapes up shore.
The waves approach out of the pressing gray.
Bands of black from the flatness beyond themselves
roll toward, and a silver light crisps their crowns.

They stretch whitely, snap to froth,
thin, and are gone—
a phrase rehearsed over and over
to the blue of beach, the pearly sea, inky sky

where I chanced to stand
foundered and numb and
waiting hours for some meaning
to break from the sand.

Golden Man*, central Asia

Who would not love the Golden Man,
as he stands effortless on the back of a winged leopard
high atop a column?
An archer, with bow to his side as in peace,
arrow shafts peek up from behind his shoulder.

Build a park about the Golden Man,
with eight bronze panels
standing for the coherence of our history.
Armies clash in the foreground,
the prisoners are taken away somewhere toward the back
near the sky.

Write songs, engrave his image on our school walls,
paint him onto our money.
We need him, to seek what he sought from on high.
We need him where we don't embrace,
where we squint to see him,
a golden plate on his chest,
the same as on the Scythians,
the moguls, the businessmen.

If we find miracles and mysteries, we give some to him:
a poem in our bones about this land erected,
wrecked and resurrected.

Our conflicted hopes,
the complexity of these streets,
are silence and wind on his back.

* The Golden Man on a winged leopard is one of the national symbols of Kazakhstan.

Val-de-Travers

To think of you is to speak in whispers
of a valley I have never seen

to breathe upon a single aster bending
in a field of asters, and touch the basic rock.

To dream of you is to roam mind's-eyed
everywhere that deep haunt.

Were the thunder to shout,
the echo would play

like harps upon each stone, nod like leaves
in idle branches moved by an inkle of light.

Colors that tip the trees
hunger for light, push forward their

greens without relent to whatever
cups can catch them.

You are drenched of sun;
you are mostly air catching light.

When the sky is deep
violet, and the moon is half hand

I will walk in dark
step, summing what I know

from the nil-est dot of night,
from the purple flash of saxifrage.

To seek you is to dream in whispered
tongue, to speak to the cataract

that knows my traverse through the
blind valley, billowing with sound.

Conqueror bird

Here is how one gains a quiet place to roll one's mind.
Caught among the doing and the being,
have we flown sufficiently far to find our soul's center?
Who is quiet enough to see this,
and being quiet, still light enough to live life in the open?

Seagone boats touch the horizon. Their spikey tops show
how the merest bristle of mast
can limit such a looming thing—the line where sky and water
look touching, as long as the eye is wide.
These to and fro boats—
hums on the grey morning
in the margins of the day, the scribbles of motors
faintly proclaiming the doing of life.

Whatever the tangents of their courses—
wave glint, heron call, the unseen sweep of wind—
there is no herald of effort save the
slowness of their returning home.
So many paths across vast wideness—so few to port.

I have taken one, but with my eye,
turning back from sea toward seaside,
abandoning that dot of destiny I saw
just west of the merest shimmer of land, and east
of what could be as little as a tug's wake,
and as much as a tide's tug.

What is cither's doing compared to a single lone
bird's eye trawling the line of sea-sky?
The conqueror bird and his glorious choice—
confines of pond to mimic mind, and there,
the bay, the world, the other side of pine.

Birds in Patancheru: a sestina

The soul battles this dazzling world; how
something small crosses a large land—
at the fence, a little green bee-eater bird—
my eye strains to trace even the frailest measure
of flight. Were you there you would have thought, in that moment,
about the birds the world does not watch

as well as this one I watch.
I stood on that parcel of India, how-
ever, to gather a list of moments
(what love, for all its capture, can't land
with such surety, nor word measure
with clear citing, as the certainty of the fleck of a bird,

at the well, night heron—by the rubbish tip, sunbird)
the whole afternoon of heat and light, to watch
the sun catching the field's fluff white like a measure
of winter. Scanning the tops of things, how
I thirst for any flit or scamper, sky to land,
to list sightings from a terrain too large for the few moments

it yields (like love, a wide excursion of waiting and moment)—
there, one, then two, coursers, then a koel—a bird
heckling in the trees, waiting to reel down and land
near the brittle mosque. Watch
these words light less well than spoonbill or drongo. How
like learning a new music; yet words can't measure

up to even the simplest well-plucked measure;
music you brought to me the moment
you perched on my long road. How
surely you turned rose my lint-colored horizon, bird
of my soul, sent as guardian of solitude to watch
over us. These lines, like long roads overland,

fare less well than bird, better than this starved, battered land,
its throngs filling the roads, flecks of color without measure.
Would I carry you, my steady love, your life and longing on my
    watch;
the pink sky and the gray of the pink breeze this moment
only flitting things; then the ashy crowned finch, babbler bird,
answering for us everything but how.

Tell us how to watch constantly high and low, how
to begin to measure from bird to bird
a land where love begs to live any moment.

Jardin des plantes

The children pose
the boats run
the trees clipped as columns
stand statuesque.
Couples promenade, and
whose ever step is that same
gravelly crush that signs us all.

The mower rounds the filial gardens
the greens now pose pondlike
in graceful terraced rings of stone.
The sound dies against the rustic wind
which shades the peonies in their pots.

That these architects, year after year, have
gotten this far!
The trees ride slowly to the sun.

Long ago, I stopped asking how did this get like this?
Questions feel like topsy, trimmed to the
aesthetic; it is what it is—
trees cropped as though
we had browsed them ourselves,
pruned to human scale.

The children with long
sticks their boats touch and turn which sail now
meeting the air anew, cast off the concrete shore
and head shoreward, the world being so round and
small. We barely launch but land.

On the Brandywine River

It has to do with being human
that we feel each eddy of the blood,
and not simply the main currents.

Our heart's design hearkens to the curls and counter-
current even as we summon intention and purpose;

it mulls with leaves in languid pools
even as we pray for moving on.

We are the strong-headed flow to sea,
even as we are multitude curlicue of rage and yearning,
small rills of pride or of regret like water over our hands.

Our currents deflect and vex
and catch the sun in their tiny maelstrom—

Oh, we wish we were all destiny,
our flood embraced within its banks.

people

Requiem

For Cynthia P.

What wants to be a hymn hangs,
foundered. We are orphan notes;
not our death, yet ours forecast,
when words submerge at last.

What was to be a song rests
unsung. We are your children cast like
shadows from light: that of you, of us becomes.

You go in emblem, like a brooch
an azure crystal set in gold
worn upon a simple coat.

Words pull us back aright;
we recount your saving deeds,
a page of notes, a card, a comb—

the simple peace in coming home.
We leave the crashing day behind
the ringing valley, lone, apart.

What mercy brings us home to you
within our souls and lets us feel
the brightened air, the cleansing storm,
and what is sung high in the heart?

Good-bye, Angel

In memory of EF Wen

We are between heaven and earth.
We know this much—
that life is a withering;
that thoughts come dry as a nutshell
to which we daily rehearse our watering;
that it is a splintering like a fern,
turning fen to forest, so green and so
proximate its humus is already in our hair.

Good-bye, Angel. You seemed
dusted-over, ready for sleep, knowing
that colors are not dreamt
but painted on a page,
words set to chisel, fanfare to flute,
touched as even the meagerest touch
of color in our deeds
helps heal the darkness
this short time.
That heaven and earth are two hands,
our lives the silence between them—
and that they clap joyous into echo.

Tell me: a daughter's dream

tell me the story of the time
when everything was so green that
green crept into the corners of night
and kept me safe as an unborn
butterfly. Tell me

when the sky was a sun-wheel
medallion, the gods were impetuous,
and lived and slept in the air
like us, soothed by the
barest of sheets. Tell me

about your footfalls on the mountain
of burning iron, your journey
toward death and back when you said
my name to the sky. Was that the moment
I was branded on your heart? Now tell me

the story of the leopard, the man-eater
who stared at you, white-eyed.
Dismissing fate, you vowed to
return to me, throwing over your shoulders
the shawl you gave me when I little,
and I flew with it as if it were wings.

My father-in-law constructs a brick step

In memory of Richard Graham

Wake up! the sun hurls itself
across the sky & with it
my soul's work at hand.

Here I will make firm land,
prepare for home this forest,
set brick to brick in the sentry light.

Resolve! the image in the mind's sight
expands to fill the space it has
with each step and reach.

The sun browses now against the leaf.
Is time attenuated, you ask,
like low tide short and shallow?

I tell you, the last slow task I allow
is a stone wheel turned upon
a pivot I design, and solve anew each day.

Take those who say
the lasting days are tide and muck
and marshy grass and tell them Go!

Go to the stone wheel!
I have seen it & have yet one
diameter left of the sun.

The voiceless

On the square mile south of Deep Neck Farm
reside a dozen of us; a mile square
in Gaza holds a thousand times thirteen souls;
in Hagadera a thousand times thirty.

Our half moon hangs above the steely bay
and katydids choir the setting sun,
and dark the pillowing clouds the far lands hold.

What path or pattern fortune formed to make
this landfall here? What history, politics, power,
war or weather converged to make this shore
line incomprehensively spare and calm,

while elsewhere the blunt press of hate, ruin of sword,
fills baskets of immiseration?
Who of us will humanize the enemy
And not be scoffed as quaint, naïve, alone?

The katydids close in, and with unvarying
volume, rhythm, edge and message sound;
and will do so for hours, nights, forever.

What can we do, with similar
relentlessness to collect our voice in this time?

Daily garage

You'd think we were the last 18 people on the last bus ride.
All you can really see is the backs of their heads, mostly.
Except for the kids—you know how they move their heads
    around the place.

The blonde girl, see, with the Cupid's bow lip.
She looks around, straight back at the large man,
who takes up two seats.

She looks at him; and you can see how we all start out like
thin blonde girl, and then grow up to take two seats.
When does that happen?

We have time to ask now, but not for long, because this is the last
    bus, the one we're taking.
Not a greyhound cross country; this one's a shuttle bus to the
    parking garage.
It will feel like an eternity, then you think: imagine if we all
    looked at each other.

Or talked like we were all coming from the same big party.
Can you imagine loving even some of these people?
That'd be your last task.
Just get to know them enough to love some.
Then you won't tire, and it won't feel like an eternity.
Get to know their stories, as many as you have time to hear, and
    you'll tell yours and it'll go like that.

Their stories surprise you, how similar.
All talking about where we parked our cars, for instance.
The human story about a simple next step.

About going to our parking spaces.
Everyone thinking about their cars, except the twin girls
and their blue suitcases all checked through to the next.

Godspeed, twin girls, you say.
You'd think this was our last ride.
How can I love all these people?

You'll figure it out.
They don't change much, really; they mostly look forward.
The man poised at the door; he thinks it's an eternity.

But I did catch his eye when he was watching me
watch the girl watch the large man. He saw that,
then our heads all turned back to regular.

perspective

A poem is a one-way horse

A poem is a one-way horse
I take out at break of day—
companion to lupine fields,
encampments, or empty wells.

The sound of dabbling water is
not packed in thought-of words,
but flow from what's written—
the salutary quaff, more or less.

The stem shrugs forth the harvest's
bale—a fragrance coils
from the promised flower.
These heartaches from the limits

on language we must bear.
The lone mare takes me to the world
that is. Its eyes are empty and black,
almost always. And I don't come back.

My lies are like a rainforest

My lies are like a rainforest
of greenish tangle-vine
& hung with humid breath—
the stolen words of mine.

My lies sprawl like rainforest
miles of verdant place—
paths like tunneled canopies
in labyrinthine space.

My lies hang like a forest top.
Macaw & monkey spy
the bees among the honey hole
the amber of my eye.

My lies employ the rainforest
to hide beneath the leaf—
the tentative explorer finds
the visit brief.

But though a path invites the eye
to walk a world untold
each step belies a hardness here,
a sound dense and cold.

The twist & shade of forest cloaks
the tundra's frosty loam—
as small the sun through winter warms
this thin green home.

Commute

The day is damp with dewy beams
the streets devoid of song
the whisper air has hints of grass
the sidewalks flow along.
Each yard encased by frilly plank
each home its walk foretells.
I'd pawn it all and cross the piers
to the place they forge the bells.

The train encases all its charge
in walls of glass and chrome
each foot is shod, each stop is rung
then silence thick as foam.
They toddle thus, and nod and read
what's new, what trends, what sells.
I ride with them but stake the path
to the place they forge the bells.

Becoming shore

the waves clasp and fold
at the point the wind meets land
in tireless cadence plash upon
though never understand

the wind, hollow, vacuous
becomes all it can
presses past what it can't find
nor feels where it began

Attention deficit

I

I doodle through
phones calls
tending each wrestling thought,
then turn to attend,

in the midst of all,
that noise, signaling a failing
appliance

in my life;
no wonder I need to read each
line twenty times;

faster, I'd burn.

How can one hold so many thoughts
in the time light takes to peel off the sun
hold its breath across breathless dark

spread itself over the world
press through eyes into the mind,
each color on arrival shouting hello?

II

The eyes also watch deaths of friends
consider the suffering world where
no light beckons; others' tremors
rattle our tea mugs; we take in
'til we shut down.

Even the sidling moon
rides gently into the corner of each night
always regarded, never forgotten,
only lost track of
so I can move again.

The cabbage line

I've always had a cabbage line
in whatever field it would take.

Each year required one, and each
year took one, ever since I was a man.

There's a lovely ease like that of
breathing to have it such:

a metered efficiency; a give,
a take of daily recompense.

My sojourn 'round the sun is
charged from this sufficient fee.

Even those days free of work have
within them constant song,

a drone of need—what it takes,
they say, to live, subsist.

The cabbage is my yoke, but also
my fief, my persistence

from which all else falls in line
and where I come to stand

And mind the sweet circumferences
from sun, crowns of green of my hand.

Poetry and truth

One is a passenger on a train;
the other a cold landscape,
trees bowed with ice sheen
leaden silver crust

but warm to the eye.
The words—they map to what's
amoebic in the mind
but are as marginal to truth

as the word fruit is to
the warm slush of peach to the tongue.
Looking out: how to remember ice like this
that seems so uncold?

Each word freezes to its space. The ice flashes by—
destined over the warm day to oblong drops.
Perhaps the two sit together in the carriage,
knees nearly touching.

One bows to write.
The other watches the trees blaze.

On Grand Cayman

A lizard is a form of life
its face as keen as a tiny man
wearing the mask of a giant,
and at war withal.

Tell me, what does it take
To gut a city of its folk, frond by
frond, until there is nothing but a curl,
Singular and unmuscular as an equation,
And then you take that away with
Your breath of fire?

Here, nothing is dire.
The ferns unfold their fractal stems.
Waves speak in diffuse dialects from a distant
source. The equation behind the cloud is as
small as a butterfly flitting in the clockwork vastness
of blue. What comes to zero in a moment rises
thunderous an hour away;
thus, is the sky so easily fresh and
eternally other.

The equations of nature are shoals of
brackets, numbers, tangents, and sums
swimming spellbound everywhere.
Men are not them:
We are fixed as lizards frozen in the sun.

I, for one, have no desire to see the world
as you say it is, as though your eye
captures more light than mine.
We will never solve for x together,
only separately, where your white-stretched waves
reach the shore and mine do not,
though they are the same wind-cast waves
our eyes rise to meet.

How to know from where
we have evolved, to whence destined?
Our forces have decamped
like a broken cloud, but
appear no other place.

Nevertheless, a solitary tern is
gliding in its private thought on windy wing
which he folds and plummets into the
azure-adopting water full of fish, or not.
It rises enough to shake itself, then takes off
at peace with its effort to get to one.

The poem is that of which it is

We are on a balcony.
Recently from the room,
we are now of the world.

A cool draft pulls the
curtains back in.
The mountain is a small up-ended

crust; the sky a waiting area
for realer colors; the few flung birds,
ancient dashes above the ocean,

a flattened shape we know goes on in
gasping distances to the left, and out.
The poem formed out of space between

breakfast's brightness and the bread
beyond the day wants wing,
wants color, wants not to be pulled back.

Why is it—why are we—stuck between
war and dance, fixed as the horizon is
fixed between color and clay?

You spoke the other day of the paradox:
je suis rassuré, yet you are filled with doubt;
sorrow for the lives of those in your sight,

the disfranchised ill, your life's work
to hope toward their aid. Can hope—
a clay shaped bowl—extend no further

than the clay itself? All becomes round;
what morphs circles the gentlest route,
to that hush at the center of time.

And what time is, is a plasmic
chaos reaching around itself
collecting what connects

and, once all is connected—
knit by purl, lintel by post, spice by broth—
warming inward to its conclusion: be it

blanket, basket, soup bowl, dwelling.
Hope is an essential ether. Khadija
folds a towel into a swan that sits

on the center of the bed. We will
change our money like we change our view,
according to a formula for swapping.

Hold it all to mind. Cancel nothing.
Wish some fantastic wish
Of half sleep, when music speaks in words.

That is what hope is, sweet repetition
of dream. Oh, to be one of those who see
all they see and look cleanly through

the vastness of doubt. The light on the vase
is the light of the vase. The flowers that
glance in the space above

are what the vase is about.
This is true from every angle,
the table being central to the room.

All my best thoughts are at this table.
Have a seat and see them.
Tell me how you want to bend the world.

why i never got
to neptune

why i never got to neptune

i left soon as i could,
turned my back to earth.

The vehicle that carried me was
fueled by what's been whispered

and all the rest as well
since the start of utterance—

all the gutturals, fricatives, all trials of sound
each attempt at understanding

each other since the first stone pit
lined up in one length and i followed,

outward toward the depth of time.
That line of narration and error and song,

words of the first thousand years freed me
from earth; bronze age i am moon-side.

Roman soldiering, every yelp from the battlefield,
from the colossus, murmurs along the wall,

line them up and there is mars.
Each year accretes more men, more women

and each of a billion children slowly learning
language: da. clah. wrr. acha.

All their collected weight,
impetus flinging me further out—

Blowery. nihil. ahnung. clahoon.
Jupiter is next, and all its moons.

Integers amass clicking over, with
each nil value, filling in

nines, eights, zeebens—
the heft of all the words approaching

a single solitary one to the left of
lone decimal, tiny punkt.

We were not yet at saturn;
streams of digits, news cycles, ripped it

from my view, leaving
behind white rings. There was no lingering

but on into unspeakable dark, a vast
of trembling and refraction.

My eyes were prisms and words
filled the space behind me, blocking what little

sun lit one last time my lids.
Young speeches, narratives, bedtime stories

tall as buildings each window lit.
Litanies, wails, lyrics of every verse sung,

six billion prayers each day
nearly completed my reach.

Looking to the neptune of the sky
i just see its blue when the final two words

reach my boat, not yet. i coast thereon,
the disk of dense and purposeful blue

grows yearly, slowly in the tiny sun that
lights its frozen solo.

Time is a slow sliding door.
Your impish satellites still as hour hands

arcing the disk of cold cobalt.
The warm ocean blue dot that you are not

faded behind. i came so far to be here.
We are both adrift. i am empty-handed.

You are as big as you will ever get
when something fails me, pressed against the dark.

THANKS

To the Delmarva Review in which "Conqueror Bird" originally appeared. DelmarvaReview.org

To my editor, Aaron Lelito, who helped me wrest from the tangle the essential threads of sound and meaning. WildRoofJournal.com

To business companions and friends, Donal O'Hare and Sharon Bean—adventures with whom and on whose behalf, helped make the world more integral, accessible, and brilliant—and to others with whom I have had the honor to travel.

To my children. When they were young, and I travelled for work, I spoke to myself their names before each takeoff and after each landing: "Andy, Hannah, Molly, Tom." Godspeed.

ABOUT THE AUTHOR

Stewart Hickman is a poet and essayist based in Maryland (USA). His previous collection of poems and short essays, *Out and Back*, was published in April 2022.

www.StewartHickman.com

www.ingramcontent.com/pod-product-compliance
Lightning Source LLC
Chambersburg PA
CBHW070452130626
46553CB00006B/2373